Families and their Faiths

Christianity in Mexico

Written by Frances Hawker and Noemi Paz
Photography by Bruce Campbell

TULIP BOOKS

www.tulipbooks.co.uk

This edition published by:
Tulip Books
Dept 302
43 Owston Road
Carcroft
Doncaster
DN6 8DA.

ISBN: 978-1-78388-013-3

Printed in Spain by Edelvives

Contents

My name is Esperanta. I have forty-nine grand-
children. This is a story about Ariceli, one of my
granddaughters. I live with Ariceli's family in a
village in Mexico.

Today we have baked a pie for Ariceli's father
and her brother, Ernesto.

'Look, here they are now!' says Ariceli. 'They're back from the hills.'

They are hungry after their long ride. Ariceli's father is a fencer. He rides around farms and checks fences. If they are broken, he mends them.

Ariceli and I both like cooking, especially pies and jams! I grow fruit in our orchard, and lots of vegetables, but sometimes we need to buy something in the village.

Like most people in Mexico, we are Christians.
We belong to the Roman Catholic Church. Our
village has a beautiful church where we worship
God. Every Sunday the family goes to a religious
celebration called Mass.

Children in Mexico go to classes every Saturday morning to learn about Christianity. This class is drawing pictures of Jesus.

God sent His son Jesus to Earth to teach people to live good lives and love each other.

8

Our village is called San Antonio. It is named
after Saint Anthony. This is his statue. Anthony
was a monk who taught people about God. He
always wore simple brown robes.

Anthony was very holy. When he died he
became a saint. Saints live in Heaven with God.

Today the Fiesta of Saint Anthony begins. It lasts for thirteen days. Every day there is a procession through the village, a Mass in the church, dancing, fireworks and a fair.

The children join in the procession. Some children dress in simple robes, just like Saint Anthony. It is very hot wearing them!

The first procession begins. A band and dancers follow noisily. Church bells ring and rockets explode. Some people believe the rockets send our prayers up to Heaven, others believe the noise scares away bad spirits.

Little Lilia puts her hands over her ears to block out the noise.

Each day the procession gets bigger as more people from other villages join in. We all thank Saint Anthony for the help he gives us, and we ask him to keep our families healthy.

When we pray to Saint Anthony we are really asking him to seek God's help.

The procession ends in the church. It is noisy during the fiesta. The band marches in, brass blaring and cymbals clashing. The church bells ring and more rockets explode into the sky.

Can you see the boy ringing the bell on the church roof? Sometimes there are four boys up there, ringing the bells to remind us to come to Mass.

Dancers enter the church. A drummer beats out the rhythm and the dancers shake rattles. Their headdresses quiver. They dance to please God and Saint Anthony and to delight the angels in Heaven.

After the Mass the priest says 'Go in peace to love and serve the Lord.'

On the way home we look at the fair in the village square. Ariceli talks to the balloon-seller's baby and buys a balloon for her cousin.

Every night of the fiesta is like a huge party. There are stalls selling toys, balloons and tasty snacks. The children enjoy the rides. Ariceli and Ernesto like the bumper cars best.

They cannot stay up too late as they have to get up early for school.

The last day of the fiesta is a special day for Ariceli. Today she will receive her first Holy Communion during Mass. She gets up early and puts on a beautiful dress and tiara. She wears make-up for the first time.

All the children who are going to take their first Holy Communion are dressed in white. They line up at the church door. The church is so full that many people have to stand outside.

As I sit and wait I look at the picture of Jesus at the Last Supper. This was the last meal He ate with His friends, the disciples, before He died. He blessed some bread and wine and asked the disciples to eat and drink in memory of Him.

This was the very first Communion. We repeat this at Mass to remember Jesus.

The priest blesses us all and begins to celebrate Mass. We sing hymns and pray together. The priest reads from the Bible, our holy book. Some children take gifts of bread and wine to the altar.

Then Holy Communion begins. Ariceli is nervous. When it is her turn the priest dips a small piece of bread into the wine and offers it to Ariceli to eat.

Now Jesus is truly with her. She has received her first Holy Communion.

Before we go to the last night of the fiesta, Ariceli and I pray together. We thank God for everything He has given us, and ask Him to look after our family. We give Him special thanks for Ariceli's first Communion.

By nightfall the village square is packed. People eat, drink and dance. Then at midnight fireworks explode over the church.

As we wander home Ariceli says, 'I'm glad I can now receive Communion every week at Mass.'

Notes for Parents and Teachers

Christianity began around 2000 years ago in the Middle East. Christians follow the teachings of Jesus Christ. They believe that He is the Son of God, sent to Earth to teach people about God. They celebrate the festival of Christmas every year to mark His birthday, and also celebrate Easter to commemorate His death. Christians believe that Jesus died to make the world a better place and to give people hope for the future. After He died, Jesus rose again and went up to Heaven to live with God.

Christians believe in the Holy Trinity: God the Father, God the Son and God the Holy Spirit. God is the Holy Father and Christians are members of His family.

The Christian holy book is called the Bible. It has two parts: the Old Testament and the New Testament. The New Testament contains the four Gospels, written by some of Jesus' followers, called the disciples.

Page 7

People go to Mass at varying times. Esperanta goes to Mass nearly every day of the year. Ariceli always goes on Sunday.

Jesus is usually shown on a cross because He died on a cross. This is called the crucifixion. The cross reminds Christians that He died for them in order to make the world a better place. You can see Him on the cross on the left-hand side of the altar in the picture on page 7.

Jesus' father was God, but His mother was a woman called Mary. She is very important to Christians. There is a statue of Mary on the right-hand side of the altar in the picture on page 7.

Mexicans hold a special affection for Mary. They believe in the Virgin of Guadalupe. The Virgin of Guadalupe is Mary, the Mother of Jesus, as she appeared to a poor Mexican farmer many years ago.

As the story of the Virgin's appearance spread across Mexico, millions of ordinary people started believing in God and became Christians. The Mexican people believe that her appearance was a special miracle for them because she spoke the same language as the farmer and looked like them.

Page 9

Saints are important in Christianity. Every town and village in Mexico has a special saint. Saints are now in Heaven with God, but once they were very holy people who lived on Earth.

When Saint Anthony was a young man, he decided that he wanted to devote his life to God. Although his family was rich, he joined the Franciscan monks who promised to live simply and to help poor people. Anthony was such a great teacher that he travelled around to spread the word of God.

Franciscan monks still wear the brown robes that Anthony wore.

Pages 12 to 15

Day after day in the hot dusty afternoon the people follow the processional cross through the village. Along the way people join the procession or watch, pray and give thanks to Saint Anthony as his statue is carried past. Young children scatter brightly coloured confetti and flowers onto the cobblestones in front of the saint. It is a long, hot walk up and down the rough cobblestone streets of the village.

Pages 16 and 17

Inside the church the band plays a song that is often sung on saints' days and birthdays:
    'I would love to be Saint John
    I wish I could be Saint Peter
    Then I could come to you all and sing
    With the beautiful music of Heaven.'

Page 25

Before the priest reads the Gospel everyone prays, 'The Lord be in my mind, on my lips and in my heart. Amen.' They make the sign of the cross with their thumb on their forehead, on their lips and over their heart.

During Mass the Creed is also said. It reminds Christians of what they believe in. It starts, 'We believe in one God, the Father, the Almighty, maker of Heaven and Earth, of all that is seen and unseen.' Then they pray for the world, for the Church and for all people.

Glossary

Angel	A Heavenly being
Bible	The Christian holy book
Fiesta	A festival
Headdress	Decorated covering for the head
Heaven	The place Christians believe people go after they die
Holy Communion	A celebration of the Last Supper. The Body and Blood of Jesus appears in the bread and wine
Hymn	A religious song
Mass	A prayer celebration held in a church. It includes Holy Communion
Monk	Somebody who leads a life devoted to God in a monastery
Procession	A group of people walking together
Roman Catholic	The Christian Church whose leader on earth is the Pope
Saint	A special person who is close to God in Heaven

Index